Presented to:

_____

From:

_____

Date:

_____

A mother's love,
With what can it compare?
It's a gift from God,
That we get to share.

JOANNA LOVELACE

kisses

from a *Mother's* *Heart*

Heartwarming Messages
That Express a Mother's Love

HOWARD BOOKS
A DIVISION OF SIMON & SCHUSTER

New York   London   Toronto   Sydney

Our purpose at Howard Books is to:
- *Increase faith* in the hearts of growing Christians
- *Inspire holiness* in the lives of believers
- *Instill hope* in the hearts of struggling people everywhere

  Because He's coming again!

Published by Howard Books, a division of Simon & Schuster, Inc.
1230 Avenue of the Americas, New York, NY 10020
www.howardpublishing.com

HOWARD

Kisses from a Mother's Heart © 2007 by Dave Bordon & Associates, LLC

ISBN-13: 978-1-4165-5855-2
ISBN-10:   1-4165-5855-1

10 9 8 7 6 5 4 3 2 1

Manufactured in the United States of America

For information regarding special discounts for bulk purchases, please contact: Simon & Schuster Special Sales at 1-800-456-6798 or business@simonandschuster.com.

Project developed by Bordon Books, Tulsa, Oklahoma
Project writing and compilation by Christy Phillippe in association with Bordon Books
Edited by Chrys Howard
Cover design by Greg Jackson, Thinkpen Design

Introduction

A kiss. It's short. Sweet. And packed with love. That's what *Kisses from a Mother's Heart* is all about. Each page of this book is a message filled to overflowing with the love I have for you, my child. As you read, I hope you'll experience that love, that you'll know how special you are, and that you'll realize how much joy I find in being your mom.

Children are a gift from the LORD;

they are a reward from him.

PSALM 127:3 NLT

You, my dear child,
are my greatest gift.

I've loved you since you were born,

and from that time,
    you have **amazed** me!

Those sparkling eyes,

tiny fingers and toes,

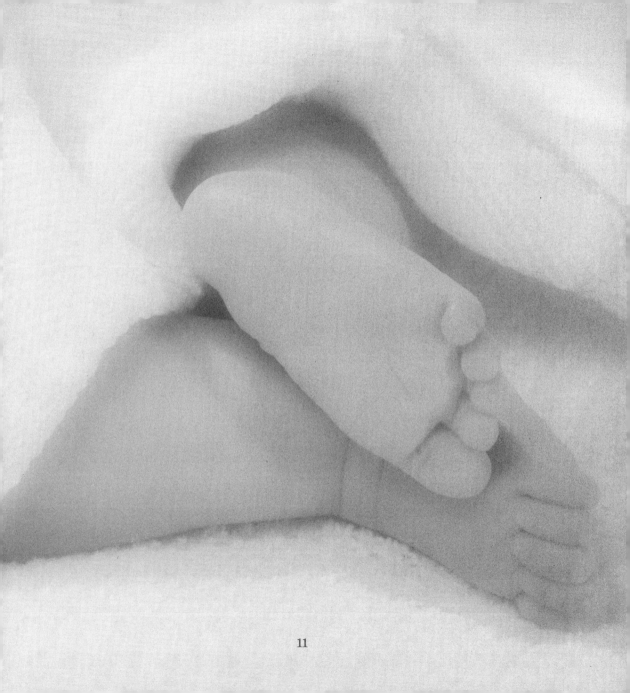

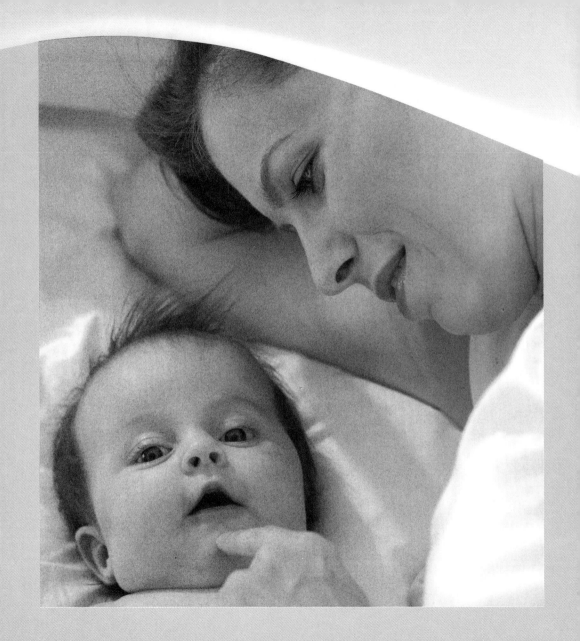

that precious dimple,

and charming smile . . .

everything about you was—
and still is—a delight!

As you grew older . . .

taking your first steps . . .

learning your ABCs . . .

losing your first tooth . . .

I knew that God had a **special plan** for your life.

You are so unique . . .

unlike anyone else in the
whole world!

And no one could ever take
your place in my heart.

I have cherished every moment

spent with you . . .

even the pouting . . .

and the tears . . .

especially the tickle sessions . . .

taking walks together · · ·

and the bedtime stories.

You've always been so kind
and thoughtful . . .

so full of life . . .

and so much fun to be around!

You've brought me so much joy.

I know you may not have
liked some of the things I asked
you to do . . .

like eat your vegetables . . .

take a time-out . . .

brush your teeth . . .

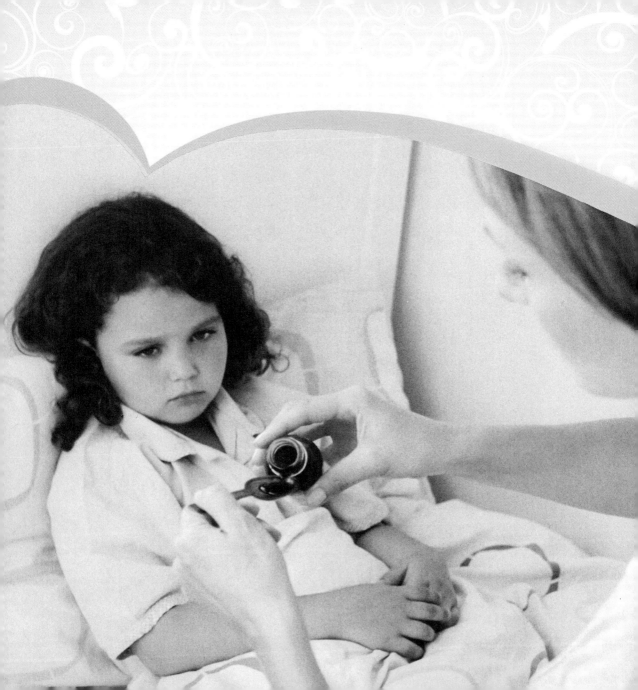

drink the cough syrup . . .

or do your homework . . .

but you always did them
with a smile—

at least most of the time!

You never failed to listen to my advice:

Don't forget the sunscreen.

There's always enough to share.

Life may not be fair,
but God's still good.

Remember to be grateful
for all your blessings.

I hope I've prepared you well for life,

and that all your
dreams come true.

And I hope you know
how proud I am of you—

of your amazing gifts
and talents . . .

of your love for God . . .

and of the beautiful person you're
becoming every day.

No matter where
the road of life takes you,

I will always be here

for you—

ready to listen,

ready to laugh,

ready to hug,

and ready to bake your favorite cookies
if you've had a bad day.

You are a priceless treasure,

and in my heart, you will always
have a home.

You have brightened my life
in so many ways . . .

through sunshine and rain.

And in you, I see the past . . .

the present . . .

and the future.

It's been the delight
of my life . . .

to call you my child.

LOOK FOR THESE BOOKS

Kisses of Comfort

Kisses of Encouragement

Kisses from a
Friend's Heart

Kisses of Love

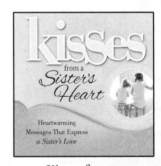

Kisses from a
Sister's Heart

HOWARD BOOKS
A DIVISION OF SIMON & SCHUSTER
New York   London   Toronto   Sydney